THE I HATE THE F
OFFICIAL HAND

THE AUTHORS

MALCOLM SCOTT

Malcolm Scott was born in London in 1954. He admits to having spent part of a misspent youth living in Paris, although he prefers the word 'existing'. He once negotiated the return of his passport from an Algerian pickpocket with a Fray Bentos steak and kidney pie. On New Year's Eve 1971 he provoked a charge by the CRS riot police.

DENISE THATCHER

Denise Thatcher has spent many years observing the French from a position of unusual influence. On her retirement in 1990 she felt able for the first time to distil her thoughts and impressions, the result being this extraordinary book.

Denise is married with two grown-up children and lives in London.

Illustrations by Martin Baker

THE
I HATE THE
FRENCH
OFFICIAL
HANDBOOK

DENISE THATCHER
& MALCOLM SCOTT

ORIGINALLY PUBLISHED IN
SEVENTEEN VOLUMES

ARROW

Published by Arrow Books Limited
20 Vauxhall Bridge Road, London SW1V 2SA

An imprint of Random House UK Ltd

London Melbourne Sydney Auckland Johannesburg
and agencies throughout the world

First published 1992
Reprinted 1993

© Malcolm Scott 1992

Printed and bound in Great Britain by
The Guernsey Press Co. Ltd
Guernsey, C.I.

ISBN 0 09 913001 7

This book is dedicated to:
my mother, Roon, Janet and Morgan.

With thanks to:
Esmerelda, Quasimodo, Simon Bowden,
Diane Davenham, Jonathan Goodman, Celestria Hales,
Mrs Lim-Cooper, Peter Silver Esq, Brian McCabe,
Jane Snell, Celia Fletcher.

and special thanks to:
Ian McLaren for his mastery of wine,
Dave Whelan for his mastery of whisky and
Peter Kenworthy for his mastery.

WARNING

Certain individuals, possibly French ones, may conceivably find one or two of the sentiments expressed in this book a bit on the strong side.

It is in no way the authors' intention to offend, attack, insult, denigrate, mock, expose or ridicule the French people except in the spirit of the warm co-operation and mutual respect that exists between our two nations.

The Gallic sense of humour is legendary throughout Europe, the Americas, indeed the whole world. We all know Claude can take having his toes tickled, in fact he welcomes it.

Onward then to the land of bidets and Bonaparte, to that mighty republic where the suppository is routinely prescribed for earache …

BRE

Why you should read this book now

FOREWORD BY BRIGADIER GENERAL SIR NORRIS
BLAKEMOOR B.O.A.C., U.H.T.

Our proud island race has seen off its quota of foes over the past thousand or so years. The inquisitive Spaniard, the jack-booted Hun – both found Albion's door securely bolted against their criminal incursions; her shutters pulled tight to their ungodly onslaughts.

On October 21st 1805 another threat was scotched, that of the upstart Boney – a French corporal with ideas above his station (Waterloo). His ships were routed in the Bay of Trafalgar and England could sleep peacefully once more.

And yet, despite these triumphs the sanctity of our shores is again under threat and threatened to boot from the same foul quarter whence sprang Napoleon.

Not only do the French, abetted by certain traitorously misguided Englishmen, seek to build an underwater causeway between our two lands, but they also plot to rip away great swathes of the fabric of our economic and cultural life. A fabric woven over the centuries by our nation's noblest minds; a fabric stained with the sacred blood of Empire. A cloth so rich and pure it makes the Bayeux tapestry look like a single ply Kleenex.

It is therefore a matter of the most imperative urgency that all like-minded Englishmen be aware of the menace. I say 'Briton, know thy enemy that he may be crushed. Understand his low schemes that they may be foiled. Learn of his ways, however unsavoury they may be, for the price of ignorance is slavery and Britons never never never shall be slaves.'

Wake up England, read this commendable and objective book and mark well its words.

MAFEKING, WILTSHIRE

Introduction

*T*he French have always felt jealous of and inferior to the English. They are quite right to do so.

Racial prejudice is often said to be a function of ignorance: the less we know of a race the more likely we are to fear and dislike them. Plausible though this theory may appear, it breaks down when we begin to examine the French. To know them is to despise them. To know them well is to discover the true nature of treachery, cowardice and barbarism.

This book is dedicated to the fearless Englishman who was asked for his papers in Les Halles – a vast concrete hole in the centre of Paris resembling a nuclear power station manned by crack-dealing punks. He handed the gendarme his copy of the *Daily Telegraph* and was promptly locked up for insolence. Well done sir!

> *I do not dislike the French from the vulgar antipathy between neighbouring nations, but for their insolent and unfounded airs of superiority*
>
> HORACE WALPOLE, 1787

50
First-class
REASONS TO HATE
THE FRENCH

PART ONE

1. The Metro
2. Boules
3. Putting an 'e' in Concorde
4. Calais
5. *Hypermarchés*
6. Perrier water
7. Le Crunch
8. Le Pen
9. Eating small birds
10. *Le boulevard périphérique*

The French Character

The French have no character – that is their distinguishing characteristic. They are spineless, emotional, weeping women to a man. They cannot speak without appearing to conduct an orchestra. They shout, they barge, they dither and they squirm. They have long puffy red noses and drink Calvados for breakfast. They drive appallingly and on the wrong side of the road. Seldom do they wash or shave, attempting to mask their odours with garlic and some 360 varieties of smelly cheese.

Scores of thousands of their womenfolk sell their bodies in narrow streets. The men who profit from this trade eat horsemeat and larks.

*T*here's rather a lot of it, as you might expect with a lippy lot like the Frogs, so let's cut to the chase and get to the so-called good bits –

Great Moments

IN FRENCH HISTORY

PART 1: THE FRANKS

When the Romans quit Gaul after 500 years, numerous tribes moved in to fill the vacuum. One thinks of the Vandals and the Visogoths, the Burgundians and the Britons, the Gascons, the Lombards and the most successful vacuum fillers of all, the Franks. Ranks of Franks sprang down across the Rhine. Their King Clovis – so called because he would eat nothing but cloves of garlic between slices of Hovis – was a tremendous unifier and alliance maker. He married a niece of the Burgundian King Gundobad and eliminated the fragrant kingdom of Cologne, some say by being there.

On his death Clovis' domains were divided equally between his four sons. This proved a recipe for 50 years of civil war but also a blueprint for the future. Time and again the Frankish kingdom was split between quarrelling sons, usually numbering four, who rejoiced in such names as Chlotar, Sigebert and Clodomir. On and on runs the badly scripted soap opera that is French history past the likes of Dagobert, Charles Martel who, we are told, encouraged missionary activity and Pepin III the Short. And so to one of those 'glorious' phases that the French seem to enjoy every thousand or so years. The reign of Charlemagne.

Now he started off with two big advantages, a dwarf for a father and only one brother who soon died. Charlemagne conquered an enormous number of places becoming undisputed master not only of France as we know it today but also of Italy, Germany, Holland and the odd bit of Spain. The late 700's were bumper years. He created the Vatican, deported large numbers of Germans from Saxony and installed his son as King of Italy. One question remained unanswered, what to give himself for a turn of the century Christmas present. Charlemagne decided not to hold back. On Christmas day 800 he had Pope Leo III crown him Roman Emperor, the first time anyone had tried that one on for 324 years.

After Charlemagne things rapidly fell apart. Louis the Pious took over but made the mistake of having four sons, among them Charles I the Bald. This was a period when a gang called the Normans first made their presence felt, it was also the heyday of the ridiculous name. Charles I the Bald had a son, Charles II the Bald, who was forever plotting with Louis the Stammerer. The situation was complicated by power hungry magnates such as Vulgrin and Boso, Count of Vienne. They in turn had to contend with Charles the Fat and Charles the Simple, the Laurel and Hardy of the first millenium.

Inside the French

A Frenchman's favourite organ is his stomach. Everything that enters and leaves as well as the manner of its coming and going is of the most abiding importance to Johnnie Gauloise. To a man they are obsessed with food, drink and bowel movements. The most commonly prescribed treatment in their hospitals and surgeries is the suppository. Why is this so?

I personally believe that Louis XIV has much to answer for. You will learn more of him in due course, suffice it to say for the moment that it was considered an immense honour to participate in the Sun King's morning evacuation ceremonies. As he was a man capable of eating six chickens at a single sitting and whose stomach was found at his death to be twice the normal size, these ceremonies one imagines were liable to be lengthy.

Most Frenchmen are closet royalists. It is their desire to possess and cultivate a stomach along the lines of a pre-war racing Bentley: one able to cruise majestically through the most tortuous banquets, one needing little maintenance and yet an anti-social beast in terms of both noise and emission control. When a Frenchman fancies a shot of just about any spirit or liquer it's odds on he'll ask for a digestif. The chances of this settling his stomach are remote and he knows it. He frankly likes to hear his belly rumble and grumble, to dwell amongst his own noxious gasses, to be reminded of the richness of his recent feasting.

This same desire to bring to public attention that which is best left unuttered, this glorification of the gut is also observable in their lamentable plumbing arrangements. To English ears and noses the typical French hotel or restaurant has all the charm of a badly run zoo. To them each gurgle and waft is a happy reminder of the digestive process. Moral: Eddie Eiffel would far rather you kneed him in the groin than punched him in the stomach.

> *France is a place where the money falls apart in your hands but you can't tear the toilet paper*
>
> BILLY WILDER

Heroes
OF THE REPUBLIC

The Marquis de Sade, 1740–1814

A deeply misunderstood victim of his own publicity and a classic case of arrested infantile development. All his efforts to attract the attention of his mother (Sexy Sadie), had the opposite effect and she had him locked up under a handy system called *lettres de cachet* (which would have formed part of the latest Tory manifesto had Margaret Thatcher not lost her grip). Because of this the Marquis spent most of his life behind bars writing shocking books of such interminable length that even today no one can bear to read them. Gave his name to an 'ism' which is more than most of us manage. In private life a real marshmallow who couldn't get to sleep without a night light.

MADAME IS A LITTLE TIED UP, BUT SHE WILL SEE YOU NOW.

COMING!

Great Moments
IN FRENCH HISTORY

PART 2: THE NORMALS

The Normals or Normans as they are sometimes known were the hard men of their day. Some put it down to the centre piece on their helmets – the squint-inducing nose protector. Who can take an opponent seriously when he goes to such lengths to protect his nose?

The Normals, it has been discovered, wore two pairs of socks on winter campaigns and put on fresh culottes before battle. They drank warm horse piss laced with calvados by way of elevenses.

The fourteenth of October 1066 was not such a great day for UK plc. If King Harold had read his stars that morning they might have said something like: 'A good day for tackling those chores around the house. If you've been ignoring your partner recently, why not take her out for a slap-up spit roast or better still, stay in. If you must engage in any outdoor activity, wear goggles.'

Now the Normals, it must always be remembered, were not French. True they spoke French as they polished their nose protectors that fine autumn morning and yes, they had taken the night ferry from Normandy but that was strictly as far as it went. So what were these nasally-fixated pirates doing in France in the first place, I hear you clamouring to know? Well, in 911 a certain Frankish king, Charles the Simple, had simply given them a large chunk of France – a

CONTINUED

stroke of diplomatic finesse worthy of Marshall Petain. It was from this rent-free French HQ that William the Bastard, accompanied by such notables as Eustace of Boulogne, had set his sights on Britannia.

Small wonder then that King Harold was defeated at Hastings. He had probably been told that some Frenchmen were picnicking on the South Downs. As he sauntered along with his chaps to flush them out of their deck chairs, I imagine he glanced up to check on the smoke from their barbecues and… wallop, arrow in the eye, temporary breakdown in discipline, two hundred years of frantic cathedral building and French has become the national language.

Moral: The French are never more dangerous than when they have lodgers.

The Famous FRENCH

NUMBER 1:
Eustace of Boulogne
1030–1081

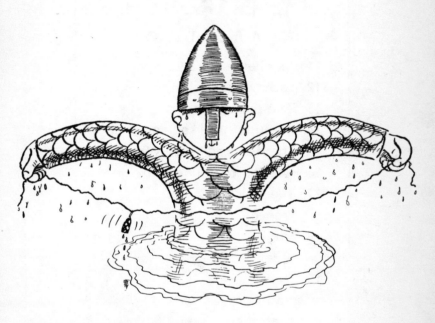

A sidekick of William the Bastard and a bit of a swine in his own right, Eustace is credited as the first man to have conceived of a fixed link across the English Channel. His plan was to put up two hyper-cathedrals, one in Boulogne, the other near Dover and to run a sort of cable car between them using ropes and pulleys.

It was pointed out to Eustace that even in a gentle breeze the passenger basket would be hurled about with great violence. To this he replied: 'We are Normans, do we not have nose protectors?'

50
First-class
REASONS TO HATE THE FRENCH
PART TWO

The Filthy French

You don't have to be a rabbi in an operating theatre to get a strong whiff of the fact that your average Frog does not consider cleanliness and godliness to walk hand-in-hand. On the other hand perhaps that is exactly what he does feel, the slight snag being that the average Frog is a miserable heathen.

Big shampooers the French are not. Only 18% of them use the stuff more than three times a week compared to a healthy 63% of the British. When they do resort to washing their lank and appallingly cut hair, they do it over the bath. Not in the bath you notice, or over the basin, no, Johnnie Gauloise likes to wash his hair over the bath because otherwise he'd never use the thing at all.

And what about conditioners? I hear you demanding to know. Do Claude and Claudette hope to compensate for their shampoo-free existence by generous use of such ancillary haircare products? No, they do not. A staggering 41% of the French, compared to 10% of the British, never use conditioners at all, making them head and shoulders Europe's most out of condition race.

Similar sorry tales come to light if we look at* soap, toothpaste, deodorants and other cleansing agents commonly associated with the second half of this century. The inescapable conclusion is that the French are indelibly filthy. Why is this the case? Why should one group of people attach such low priority to personal hygiene compared to their immediate neighbours? There are, I believe, several reasons.

For a start the French live in a large and underpopulated country and so, quite simply, they run into each other less often

* The French look at them too, but that's as far as it goes.

than the average European. Then there is the 'peasant factor' to take into account. For reasons best known to themselves, large numbers of Frenchmen, who in any other country would be called farmers, cling to the notion that they are in fact peasants. A peasant wears blue overalls and potters in a large Mercedes between his tiny plot of land and the local post office where regular and generous subsidies from the British taxpayer await him.

Being a peasant these days is becoming a harder and harder business. His desire to do things in the time honoured way is continually jeopardised by labour-saving machinery and pesticides. The less the peasant grows, the more he makes and the more he makes the harder it is for him to feel like a true blue peasant. One solution to this identity crisis, or 'peasant anxiety syndrome'[†] as it has become known, is to smell like a peasant. After only a few days of not washing he notices the queue in the post office evaporate before him; animals become his close friends. True it can be a lonely existence but at least the 'peasant' can now live with himself (and avoid costly psychotherapy).

Whilst the above factors may go some way to explain rural smelliness, they cannot excuse the fearful bombardment of the nose that any Englishman receives in a typical French city. In warm weather one can find oneself praying to be struck down by a severe cold. To inhale deeply in a Parisian metro carriage during a July rush hour is the act of a man who is tired of life. It is to travel through time and space – approximately to the Middle East in the middle ages. The ultimate blackspot on the metro system is where the line passes under the Seine at Chatelet. In an economy drive of breathtaking shoddiness the tunnel is made to double up as a main sewer. Even the French find this stretch a little testing.

And here, I believe, we arrive at the meat of the matter. Quite simply, the French smell things differently to you or I, if they smell them at all. They are not offended, put out, bothered or

† See Brian Damage, *Peasants, Personality & Pollution*, Strathclyde University Press, 1954.

fazed by smells that just about any other human being would find perfectly scandalous. The word 'merde' is one of the most commonly used in the French language. This is because they cannot smell what they are talking about, or if they can they do not mind. The peculiar shape and puffiness of the French nose may play some part in this, but for those who still doubt my theory ‡, I will let my case rest on three further arguments.

Firstly, it should be mentioned that so far in this admittedly short piece I have not once used the word garlic. In the time a Frenchman would have taken to read this he would have wolfed down an average of 1.3 cloves. Secondly, there is the fact to consider that over fifty million French people live in France. I put it to you that mass emigration is only avoided by severe shortcomings in the French nasal department. To put it another way, unless nose-wise they are non-starters, how can they bear to live there? Finally, I will ask you a question. To the best of your knowledge has there ever been a 'dirty protest' in a French prison? No, because nobody would notice. I rest my case.

‡ See Brian Damage, *Gallic Olfactory Deficiency*, University of Buffalo Press, 1956.

The Famous FRENCH

NUMBER 2:
Auguste Bidet 1641–1689

August 1672 was a scorcher and the young Auguste Bidet was suffering acute social embarrassment. No washerwoman would take in his intimate garments and even the cheapest whores would cross the boulevard at his approach.

Bidet dangled himself for long hours in flasks of iced rosewater. He shaved his loins, massaged costly jellies into his unmentionables, but all to no avail. Until one night, in a flash of odorous tumescence, he sketched the patent for the vessel which would assure the Bidet name of immortality.

Unfortunately, while testing an early prototype of his 'intimate cleansing machine', Auguste impaled himself upon a shard of glass, all but severing his links with the male of the species. He died a wealthy but broken man seventeen summers later.

The Hundred Years War

The Hundred Years War lasted officially from 1337 to 1453 (116 years). In the opinion of many respected commentators it was a good deal too short. There was no sport more enjoyed by English medieval kings than waging campaigns on French soil, in fact since the arrival of the Normals we'd been beating up on Johnnie Gauloise pretty much continuously. The usual excuse for Frog-bashing, as though we needed one, was that large chunks of France were ours and for some extraordinary reason they didn't like it too much. Come 1337 though we hit on a new wheeze; Edward III of England claimed the French throne.

The first big dust-up came at Crécy in 1346. Edward had landed with 10,000 men in Normandy and was happily pillaging the countryside when Claude showed up with 20,000 of his finest. Edward ordered his cavalry to dismount, formed them up in three battalions on the crest of a hill and placed archers on the flanks of each battalion. The French knights charged all day but never got close, well, only within longbow range. After tea it was our turn to bat. We swept majestically down the pitch and wrought merry havoc until bad light stopped play.

The second test occured at Poitiers twenty years later. This time we were captained by Edward's son the Black Prince who employed the same tactics as at Crécy. Strangely enough so did the French. Two thousand of their knights took an early bath; an equal number were taken prisoner, among them the French King. This proved to be a valuable wicket. Gaul degenerated into anarchy while they passed the hat round to collect his enormous ransom. Needless to say we never saw the money and I for one would be interested to know what it worked out to these days, allowing 625 odd years inflation and interest.

Serious play was suspended for many years due to the Black Death but in 1415, Henry ('once more into the breach dear friends') the Fifth took a team of 8,000 on a tour of Normandy. The French captain Charles VI was insane and had been substituted by the Count of Armagnac, a man it seems with such a bad hangover that he had completely forgotten the lessons of the previous century, particularly with regard to galloping uphill towards men with bows and arrows. Oh dear, oh dear, oh dear. Armagnac led 25,000 glittering knights on to the field of Agincourt... and very few of them back to the pavilion.

After this the French stopped playing cricket and relied instead on the inspiration of an illiterate teenager called Joan. It was thoroughly disconcerting, as though Saddam Hussein had suddenly got Kylie Minogue to head up the Republican Guard. The English rapidly lost interest in matters French and we decided to let them keep the place.

28

THE JOAN OF ARC

RAP

I heard my first voice when I was thirteen
I was just going to lay down with some Ovaltine
It said 'Go see the Dauphin
'Cos he ain't havin' no fun
And, baby, you're the one
*   to put him back on the scene'.*

Next thing I know I'm in a suit of armour
Now that can sure do some weird things
*   to your karma*
We win some ground
I get the Dauphin crowned
Hey, this ain't right – I'm the
*   daughter of a farmer.*

Well, things were cool until
*   one day*
I got framed by the Bishop
*   of Beauvais*
He made a big mistake
They burnt me at the stake
But now I'm a saint 'n it's
*   heaven all the way.*

The Famous FRENCH

NUMBER 3:
Marcel Accord
1725–1781

The son of a fan-gilder from Avignon, Marcel was born profoundly deaf. After a pilgrimage to Lourdes the family believed him to be cured of his affliction and enrolled him in the local conservatoire of music and arts. Although a willing pupil, Marcel's main accomplishment was to successfully turn the pages of his fellow students' sheet music at concerts. In fact, there were always doubts about Marcel, especially when he began to boast about what he called his 'portable organ'.

Aggroculture

*T*he French farming 'community' is addicted to *manifestations* or, in plain English, riots. If you can't sell your produce at a high enough price, you find someone to blame – usually *le gouvernement* – and then you take to the streets. *C'est la guerre!*

A LOAD OF MANURE

The French farmer will extract money from the government as follows: he takes a thousand or so tractors to Paris and drives around slowly in the rush-hour traffic. Then he dumps a few loads of manure on the steps of the Elysée Palace and pops in to collect his cheque. If, by some cunning means the Ministry manages to blame Brussels instead and refuses to cough up, then the whole charade is repeated at border posts, holding up exports for a few days.

ROAST LAMB

When the British began to export English lamb to France in 1990 they put the *chat* firmly among the *pigeons* and climbed straight up the *nez* of the French Aggro-lobby. In France only the most prestigious restaurants can afford the best lamb – the *pré-salé* animals from the salt marshes of the mouth of the Loire and the Gironde. As a rule, French lamb comes from the dry hills of the interior and is scrawny, over-priced and has suffered badly from drought. Now French housewives rushed to buy the tender English meat…

Naturally the French farmers joined the battle, they blockaded a few ports and waited for the Brits to give up and go away.

Then the perfidious Albions began to take lorries full of live sheep into every port, driving across France to the abattoirs. *Quel horreur!* Hence the road-blocks and informal barbecues. It was Agincourt all over again.

BRUT FORCE

There is a long tradition of civil disobedience in the Frenchman's peasant soul. The best-known manifestation in the wine trade took place in 1911, in Champagne. For years there had been complaints of wine being 'imported' into the region and then passed off as the real thing. Then came a run of bad harvests and in 1910 there was almost no crop at all. The growers were in distress but, suspiciously, the wine-merchants still had Champagne to sell. The rioting began in January. Premises were vandalised, shipments of wine were attacked and barrels adulterated with paraffin. The government tried to make peace and only made things worse. The riots spread. The army was called in but even a cavalry charge could not prevent cellars being sacked. The mayhem continued until April when order was finally restored. Only Bollinger was spared…

To this day the CRS, the notorious French riot police, refuse to control demonstrations in wine-growing regions.

> *Here's to Champagne, the drink divine*
> *That makes us forget our troubles.*
> *It is made of a dollar's worth of wine*
> *And three dollar's worth of bubbles.*
>
> ANON

Heroines
OF THE REPUBLIC
Brigitte Bardot, 1934–

Studied engineering at Wolverhampton Polytechnic and went on to make several 'beach' movies, including Twin Castles, Sheltered Inlets and perhaps her classic, Please can you rub this into my shoulders, Alain.

In 1974 she opened a suntan lotion shop in St Tropez and began a secret affair with Idi Amin's younger brother, Yehudi. Although awarded the *Legion d'Honneur* in 1981, Brigitte Bardot has never visited South Wales. She is immensely kind to animals and currently looks after fourteen stray cats, a baboon and a colony of head lice.

Great Moments
IN FRENCH HISTORY

PART 3: THE FRENCH REVOLUTION

It was, as they say, a good time to keep your head down…
France in 1789 was in bad shape. The country was bank-
rupt, the winter was severe, the previous year's harvest had
failed and bread prices were sky high. Ruling not-so-divine-
ly was the vacillating Louis XVI, married to Marie-
Antoinette who, in the circumstances, would have been
better off not recommending cake to the poor.

The Revolution lasted six years, becoming increasingly
bloodthirsty as successive waves of reformers seized power
and executed the previous batch. In the process nearly all the
luminaries of the period, including the Royal Family, Marat,
Danton and Robespierre, were slaughtered. Consequently
the most significant personality of the era may well be the
humanitarian doctor, Joseph-Ignace Guillotin, inventor of a
machine capable of separating the head from the body 'in
less time than it takes to wink'. During the period of terror,
in 1793/94, some 2690 winks would have been required to
measure the guillotine's productivity.

In the midst of this carnage, Frenchmen made important decisions. They imposed a Revolutionary Calendar,
forced priests to marry as part of a 'dechristianizing' process
and replaced Saints' Days with festivals in favour of the
pumpkin and the dungheap. It must have been a relief
when, in October 1795, a young artillery general called
Bonaparte turned up.

Sex

*F*renchmen as a rule do not enjoy having sex. This is why their women have always had to go to such strenuous lengths to make themselves appealing. The trouble with sex, as far as Claude is concerned, is that it interferes with more important pastimes. To put it another way, the position of intimacy most commonly associated with the French is one in which the participants eat. Is this a coincidence? Unlikely.

On the rare occasions when a French man does feel the blood rising in his clogged veins and arteries, the chances are that it will not be his wife to whom he turns. It will be somebody else's. The adulterous couple will typically liaise in a routine known as the *cinq à sept* or the 'five to seven'. This is not a variation on the numerical position referred to above,

le croissant neuf

nor thankfully does it involve any products of the Heinz food company. *Cinq à sept* is merely what is muttered to the concierge of the shabby hotel which the eager couple have selected for their unsavoury couplings. The English equivalent – though perish the thought that an Englishman would ever resort to such behaviour – might be: 'Oh excuse me, I was wondering what the policy of this fine establishment was regarding the booking of rooms for less than the normal twenty-four hour period... a couple of hours around teatime was really what I had in mind.'

If a Frenchman has no mistress with whom to take tea, he will not hesitate to seek gratification on the streets. Prostitution is not so much a crime in France as a career. The first building to have air-conditioning in Paris was a brothel – the lavishly decorated Sphinx on Boulevard Raspail, opened just after the First World War. Every summer the working girls of Paris migrate southwards to the Cote d'Azur to man the fleshpots of Cannes and Nice. Fleshpots of quite a different nature are to be found year-round in the infamous Bois de Boulogne, wooded park land a mere mile or two from the Arc de Triomphe.* Tarts have operated here for generations but, if you go down to the woods today, you're in for a big surprise. Imagine the scene – and if you have any sense go no further – you are driving innocently through the *bois*, your head-lights pick out the unmistakeable contours of a glamorous woman who by means of lewd gestures causes you to stop. A bargain is struck and you venture from your car into the clutches of this siren of the night. She places your hand upon her generous bosom and tries to make sure you're not a policeman (if you are she knows she'll never see her money). Soon afterwards you emit a curdling yell of horror – you are touching a bloody man!

For some reason the French find it normal to have bands of Brazilian transvestites and transsexuals roaming their parks after dark. I can only surmise that they cater to some deep-seated abnormality in the French male. Word must surely have spread of the unusual characteristics of the nocturnal South American wood-folk and yet they continue to flourish. Claude seems to like surprises of this unnatural nature. You may draw your own conclusions.

* There are those who claim that Napoleon's erection of this monument had little to do with military conquest or French *gloire* and a lot to do with the Empress Josephine, a lifelong yoga enthusiast. She gave Boney a consistently hard time and he considered it a real triumph when he could get her to arch her back.

Why do the French seek sex so energetically outside the bonds of wedlock? Why are there so few sex scandals involving politicians? The reason is that having a mistress in France is rather like running a second car or joining the golf club. It is a status symbol, it is expected. If a photograph of Mitterand's mistress[†] were splashed over the front pages of the newspapers there would be a national yawn. If she was pretty he might go up a couple of points in the polls.

The rules of adulterous behaviour, how husband, wife and mistress should conduct themselves, were laid down long ago by Louis XIV. If ever there was a king of France who liked to get his leg over it was Louis. Indeed he was so rampant that he even made love to his wife once a fortnight, the plain and permanently frosty Marie-Thérèse (we know it was once a fortnight because she always took communion the following morning). In between times Louis was a goat. With Madame de Montespan he had nine illegitimate children, but she grew fat and he discarded her. Madame Scarron, her successor, complained that sleeping with Louis twice a day was having an adverse effect on her health. The poor woman was seventy-five at the time and the King five years her junior.

Louis had *grandes affaires* like the two mentioned above. He also had *petites affaires* lasting perhaps a week or a month and, just to ensure that no crevice of his kingdom went unexplored, he had regular afternoon recruitment sessions where fresh faces lucky enough to have caught the royal eye would be given a chance to market themselves. One teenage girl who graduated successfully from afternoon to evening work was Mademoiselle de Fantagues.

Her career as one of Louis' vessels was short but to the point. Fanny had one remarkable asset, she was the most beautiful woman in France. We know this to be true from an unimpeach-

---

† Besotted though the French President evidently is with Margaret Hilda Thatcher, exhaustive research reveals this to be an unrequited passion.

able source, Louis himself, the man who for sixty years conducted a nationwide beauty contest with himself as first prize. Soon Mademoiselle de Fantagues had rendered sufficient services to the State to merit being made a duchess, but unhappily her beauty was not matched by her wit. Indeed it would probably be fair to

say that her combined brain power was worth about one of her bewitching eyelashes. Louis installed her in a little room in Versailles next to his own apartments but when they encountered one another outside the royal bedchamber he pretended not to know who she was. Perhaps she didn't mind being snubbed in this way, perhaps she didn't notice. In any case she aroused frantic jealousy, particularly from the fertile Montespan who sent her a pair of poisoned gloves. Little Fantagues took to crying and being ill which Louis could not abide. She was packed off to a convent where she died at the age of twenty, happy, it is said, because on her account the King of France had wept.

Frenchmen of letters are especially associated with lechery. Alexandre Dumas and Victor Hugo, both born in 1802, seduced women at a rate known only to the likes of 60s rock stars. Both were still rampant into old age, not to say dotage. Hugo, we are told, at the age of eighty was discovered by his grandson ravishing a laundry maid in a linen cupboard. 'Look little Georges,' he declared 'that's what they call genius.'

Alexandre Dumas was another prolific writer whose passion for passion makes it astounding that he had the opportunity to pen more than the odd short story. He claimed to have had 500 illegitimate children and lived on an estate called Monte Cristo which he turned into a sort of harem where an ongoing love-in was the order of both day and night. Dumas had the morals of a butterfly, but perhaps this was for the best. 'I need several mistresses,' he said. 'If I only had one she'd be dead inside eight days.'

A sordid triumvirate of pen-pushing French fornicators is made up by the prodigious Georges Simenon, the creator of Maigret. In terms of throughput, Georges wins trousers down. He claimed to have slept with over 10,000 women, believing that only in the throes of sexual crisis could a woman be truly understood. Georges apparently died an unhappy man. It grieved him to think of all the millions of women he had been unable to fathom.

Heroes
OF THE REPUBLIC
D'Artagnan

The only one of The Three Musketeers not to be named after an aftershave. In his various cinema manifestations D'Artagnan has been played by Errol Flynn, Ronald Coleman, Oliver Reed and of course Jerry (of Tom and Jerry) in the 1961 classic *The Three Mouseketeers.*

VIVE LE TROILISME

Foie Gras

With the possible exception of horsemeat, the one French delicacy which the RSPCA would most like to see banned is *paté de foie gras*, literally *paté* of crammed liver. The liver in question is plucked from a goose or duck around the time of the first frost. Prior to its plucking, however, the organ will have undergone a sinister transformation in a process known as the *gavage*.

> ## HOW TO GAV A GOOSE OR DUCK:
>
> 1 Take one innocent bird of the above-mentioned species.
> 2 Place it in a small box so that it cannot move.
> 3 Fashion a hole on the top of the box through which the creature's head may protrude.
> 4 Feed it intensively for three to four weeks on a diet of salted, fatty maize by means of a tube thrust down the throat.
> Note: these are pretty greedy animals anyway but the gaver's task is to get the things to over-eat, if necessary by massaging the food down its gullet.*
> 5 Wait for the first frost.

---

* It has been theorised that the French passion for *foie gras* and their calm acceptance of the gaving process is due to a subconscious desire of Frenchmen and women to meet a similar fate.

What happens is that the bird's liver swells to outrageous proportions, as much as four pounds or 370% of its original size. Were you to remove the box towards the end of the process, far from waddling off, the creature would probably keel over. The result is a rounded block of almost pure fat, as much like your normal piece of liver as is a McDonalds to a baron of Scotch beef. After a little delicate cooking the *foie* becomes unrestrainedly delicious. It glides across the tongue like mother's milk and for the few brief moments between delectation and acute indigestion you are in paradise. To make these moments last, *foie gras* is best served with plain toast and Chateau Yquem, but this isn't good enough for the French.

According to *Larousse Gastronomique* there are forty-three recognized ways of preparing *foie gras*. You may be tempted by *foie gras à la financière* – stud a *foie gras* with truffles, pour on some brandy and leave for a few hours. Cook with pork fat in a Madeira-based stock and serve on fried bread. Or maybe escalopes of *foie gras* with grapes sound more up your street, or perhaps *foie gras* cutlets, rissoles, croquettes or *medaillons*.

For a change why not plump for *foie gras* pancakes *à la périgourdine*, which calls for the addition of a little Armagnac[†]? Or *foie gras Richelieu*, a sort of battered *foie gras* sautèed in clarified butter? Still not satisfied. Why not force back some *foie gras* loaf, hot or cold, *foie gras* mousse, *foie gras* soufflé or *foie gras* inside any of half a dozen types of pastry?

Whichever way the ultra-rich, melting liver of the gorged duck or goose ends up slipping down your throat, the chances are you'll regret it, but probably not quite as much as the involuntary organ donor.

FOIE GRAS – THE FACTS

A goose in the last week or so of its life may 'consume' as much as six pounds a day of its liver-swelling mash. This is the equivalent of a human being eating twenty-eight pounds of spaghetti – without the benefit of sauce or parmesan.

Around two million geese are being force-fed in France alone. The number of force-fed Frenchmen, excluding children, is believed to be far higher.

France produces 60% of the world's *foie gras*: 2,730 tonnes in 1983.

French consumption is galloping forward by 8% per year, mainly due to more being sold in tinned form in supermarkets.

† This need not be as extravagant as it sounds. Any left over armagnac can be added to your small bird-drowning reserve, enabling you to kill two birds with one shot.

Note: such tinned products contain between 20 and 75% *foie gras* and are usually pretty grotty.

In 1984 France imported 1,500 tonnes of *foie gras*... 968 tonnes from Hungary, 200 tonnes from Israel, 160 tonnes from Poland and 80 tonnes from Bulgaria. This means that virtually all the world's *foie gras* passes through France.

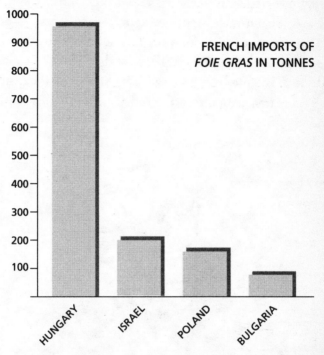

FRENCH IMPORTS OF
FOIE GRAS IN TONNES

In the same year France exported 700 tonnes of mainly tinned *foie gras*, of which it is the world's only producer. Of this 70% went to six countries, who were, in order of consumption: Switzerland, the US, West Germany, Japan, the United Arab Emirates, Great Britain.

The official British attitude is that to ban imports of *foie gras* would be contrary to the Treaty of Rome, but that the force-feeding methods used would contravene UK animal protection law. It is the same dubious stance as the government takes on Scandinavian porn – import it if you will but you can't make it here.

Name-Calling

Were you to come back to life as a Frenchman – surely one of the ultimate negative karmic experiences – do not expect an easy time of it for your first seventy-two hours. Your parents may well be preoccupied. Within three days of any Claude or Claudette's arrival, the law states that they must be given a Christian name from the official list of Gallic saints and heroes.

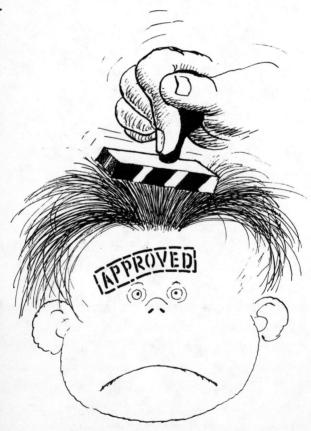

In France you cannot call your offspring Zac, Elvis or Pythagorus or name them after planets, motor cars or the cup-winning football team of the moment. No. Rather you shall refer to them as Jean-Marie, Huguette or Cyrille. Here is my personal selection of faves from the *Directoire Officielle*, promulgated by the Bureau of Gallic Nomenclature within the *Ministère de l'Interieure* authorised by article 762·3 of the *Code Napoléon*:

Boys	Girls
Albéric	Bienvenue
Baudouin	Clothilde
Bérengère	Euphrosine
Foulques	Ludivine
Gonzague	Marie-Madeleine
Pie	Sixtine
Tancrède	Théotime

The following names were chosen from a phone book, picked more or less at random for a medium-sized town that must remain anonymous. Well, suffice it to say it begins with an 'M' and lies 151 kms due west of Aix-en-Provence:

Sylvie Costargent	Agnès Orgeas
Isabelle Delafolie	Guy Phalipou
Jean-René Detour	Ghislaine Philipson
Jacques Harlot	Philippe Qualité
Florence Killing	Christine Terrible
Antoine La Rotonde	Violette Tartiére
Dr Armel Le Cat	Henri Wanko
Cyrille Naffah	Sylvie Worms de Romilly
Jean Occhiminuti	Régis Zani

Remember, you don't have to call the French names, they're managing perfectly well on their own.

The Famous
FRENCH

NUMBER 4:
Eugene Casserole
1348–1382

He was not, as many believe, a cannibalistic serial killer cum restaurateur. True, he cooked and served human flesh, but it was always dead by the time it reached Chez Casserole in uptown Montmartre.

Eugene is thought to have cooked the first black woman ever eaten in the capital. The nobility flocked to his door, although foul play was suspected when he still had *Gigot de Negresse au Beurre Noir* on the menu a whole year later.

Casserole was flung into the Bastille. There he wrote his seminal work: '101 ways to cook a rat', recently reissued in a wipe-clean microwave edition.

50
First-class
REASONS TO HATE
THE FRENCH

PART THREE

21. Hairy armpits (female)
22. Handbags (male)
23. Garlic breath (both sexes)
24. Feigned incomprehension when you talk Frog
25. Snotty waiters
26. Scrounging waiters
27. The Super Phoenix fast-breeder reactor
28. Jacques Delors
29. Minitel
30. French tea

The Foreign Legion

The Foreign Legion, or Legiron as it's sometimes known, exists for those who weren't sent away to sufficiently beastly boarding schools in their formative years. It's actually quite hard to get in these days, but if you can demonstrate previous military experience, a strong deathwish and a low IQ, the battle is halfway won.

After four weeks of intensive training, recruits are given a small saucepan to wear on their heads, otherwise known as the sacred white kepi. After six weeks they are given breakfast.

WARNING

If you are reading this page in a public place, discreetly study the faces of any men who are lurking about. The Foreign Legiron is a bit iffy about having its leg pulled, particularly on the subject of the sacred white kepi. In the interests of reader safety, this will be referred to in future as the sacred white KP.

The Legion are an elite crack force. They climb mountains (without ropes), patrol jungle rivers (without boats) and leap from aeroplanes (on commercial flights). Their real speciality though is heroic death. A legionnnaire's idea of body armour is

skin. They've died heroically on five continents and they'd like nothing better than to pick a fight with someone in Antarctica, preferably in winter.

One of the Legiron's most famous exploits occured in Camerone, Mexico, in 1863. A force of sixty-four men commanded by Capitaine Danjou was sent off to rendezvous with a large gold shipment. Unfortunately they were caught on open ground by 2,000 gold-loving and blood-thirsty Mexicans. The legionnaires, who were making coffee at the time, abandoned their espresso machines and made a dash for the shelter afforded by the hamlet of Camerone.

Here, not content with beating off cavalry charges, infantry attacks and fire-bombings, they persisted in attacking the enemy with bayonets. At eleven a.m. the Mexican commander invited them to surrender. To this proposal he received the curt reply: 'Merde.' By teatime there were just thirteen legionnaires left. When they were reduced to five in number, they charged again.

There is no relic more sacred to the Foreign Legion than the wooden hand of Captain Danjou, recovered from the battlefield of Camerone. Every year it is taken from the Legion crypt and paraded. If you really want to rub a Frenchman up the wrong way, try asking him: 'Why did Captain Danjou's wife often look flushed in the mornings? Because he made her screw on his hand'.

Heroes
OF THE REPUBLIC

Jean-Marie Le Pen, 1928–

After rising to the rank of delivery man in the French postal service, Le Pen worked at Granada's Membury service station on the M4. He was parachuted into Algiers two years after independence where he landed on a traffic cone.

This proved to be the key moment in crystallizing the Le Pen *philosophie de la vie*. 'In a flash I saw everything,' he writes in his memoirs, 'surrounded by natives, no passport, an unwanted and unwashed foreigner with but one thought in mind – to dislodge myself from this impertinent bollard.' Two years later the *Front National* was a reality. Jean-Marie was once married to a *Playboy* centrefold.

Sour Grapes

From the foil on its corks to the roots of its vines, the French wine industry is a con. A reasonably pleasant con as far as these things go but a full-bodied, no-holds-barred jeraboam of a con nonetheless.

France grows about seven and a half million tonnes of grapes per year and some twenty-two million tonnes of sugar beet. This state of affairs has more than a little to do with the action of Jean-Louis Chaptal, Napoleon's Home Secretary. In 1801 he suggested that sugar be added to fermenting wine in order to increase the alcoholic strength. Previously, strong wines from Spain and brandy had been added to make the wines fit to ship. At a stroke, Chaptal reduced imports and helped French farmers: it is a wonder that he wasn't made emperor in his own right.

Sugar is by no means the only additive you'll find in French wine. Water and acid are frequently needed after sugaring to bring the stuff back to standard strength and taste. Then of course there are the 800 million bottles of Mediterranean wine imported annually (mainly from Spain and Southern Italy) which are used to give 'French' red wines a nice dark colour.

TEN AND A HALF BILLION GREEN BOTTLES

That's how many bottles a year the French produce – about two for everybody on the planet. Well, yes – about four billion bottles a year are poured straight into the European wine lake. Of this, a tiny amount is used to make vermouth and vinegar (is there a difference?) and the rest is distilled into industrial alcohol. That still leaves six and a half billion bottles – surely that's enough to go round? Wrong.

Johnnie (rinse my dentures in Beaujolais) Gauloise slurps five and a half million bottles himself. That works out as a staggering 110 bottles per year for every man, woman and *bébé* in the land. If you exclude the very old, the very young, diabetics and one and a half million Moslems, you can begin to understand why the national affliction in France is '*crise de foie*' – a pain in the liver. This necessitates long visits to spas and health resorts (subsidised by the national health system), and means that France has one of the highest rates of cirrhosis of the liver in the world. France also leads Europe in cases of cancer of the oesophagus, another booze-related complaint.

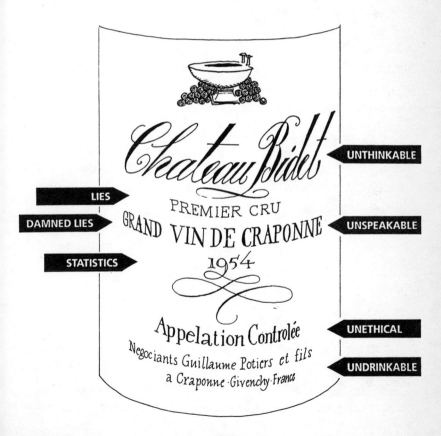

Hard Cheese

The French make around 500 different varieties of cheese including Cheddar and feta. Fifty of these congealed dairy products are protected by an *Appellation d'Origine*. This simply means that the cheese comes from a particular place. Some *Appellation d'Origine* cheeses are made in factories from pasteurised milk. Some are made from the 'wrong' type of milk, i.e. cows' milk which is often substituted for goat or sheep because it is available all year round.

Crottins

Selles

Ossau

Lagiole

Here for your delectation are some of Claude's all-time favourites in the *fromage* department:

Crottins de Charigol – tiny, hard, goats' milk cheeses with black or grey-brown mouldy rinds. Horribly sharp and salty when fully aged and intimidating to all but the most dedicated. The name means 'horse-droppings'.

Ossau Traty Brebis Pyrenées – ewes' milk cheeses weighing nine to eleven pounds, ripened for at least three months. Older cheeses have to be grated.

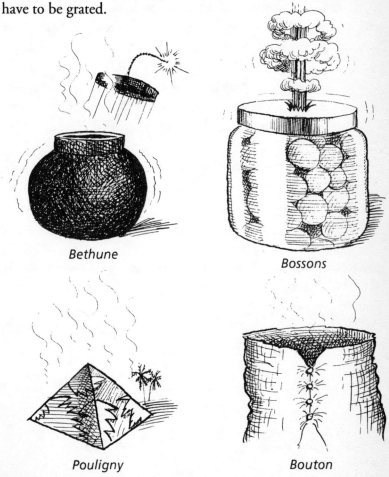

Bethune

Bossons

Pouligny

Bouton

Bethune also known as **Vieux Puant** – 'Old Stinker'. A seriously strong cheese made from *Maroilles* (a pale, full cows' milk cheese), mashed up with pepper and herbs and sealed in jars to ferment for several months. Supposedly a treat for the local Flemish coalminers, who wash it down with copious quantities of the local gin.

Pouligny St Pierre – a small, pyramid-shaped goats' milk cheese with a tangy flavour, ripened in a covering of dead leaves.

Selles de Cher – a sweet, nutty goats' milk cheese which is covered with salt and charcoal, giving it a black coating. *Selle* means stool (in the lavatorial sense).

Lagiole – huge, one hundredweight cheeses, made in Acquitaine from the milk of Aubrac cows. It has a full, fruity flavour, and after six months of ageing, is distinctly robust.

Bossons Macérés – made by soaking miniscule goats' milk cheeses in a mixture of herbs, oil and brandy for several months. It is said to be *'parfaitment abominable et bon seulement pour les snobs'.*

Bouton de Culotte – tiny goats' milk cheeses, dried for winter use: extra sharp, with a dark grey or brown rind. The name means 'trouser button'.

> **Only 23 more pages to go before French rock 'n' roll**

FIVE FRENCH
Fashion Failures

1. Berets
2. Striped T-shirts
3. Fishnet stockings
4. Culottes
5. Onions (see 1 and 2)

Great Moments
IN FRENCH HISTORY

PART 4: NAPOLEON – ACTION MAN, 1769–1821

The first thing to bear in mind about Napoleone Buona-parte is that he was only technically French. His father Carlo was of Tuscan descent and an established lawyer in Ajaccio, Corsica. Napoleone, his second surviving son, was born just fifteen months after the island was ceded to France by the Italian state of Genoa.

When the French turned up to occupy the place not unnaturally there was resistance from the natives. What did Carlo do? He joined up with the resistance. What did he do next? He collaborated with the French and became an important legal official.

At the age of nine, Napoleone along with Joseph his elder brother were shipped off to school in France where they considered themselves to be foreigners. N.B. set foot in Paris for the first time when he was fifteen to attend the mil-itary academy. He passed out a year later – the first Corsican to do so – and became a second lieutenant in the artillery.

His first impulse was to return to Corsica and he made several trips there between mainland postings. Two facts from this period stick in the mind. In January 1792 he was listed as a deserter by the French and in April '93 the Corsi-cans, who Napoleone was trying to 'revolutionize', con-demned the Buonaparte family to 'perpetual execration and infamy' at which they all fled to France.

The next few years were to prove frustrating, though possibly character-forming, for the skinny young gunner. He lived mostly in cheap hotels in Paris. He joined the Jacobin Club and used to make rabid speeches denouncing the clergy and aristocracy. His big break came with the end of the Revolution. The royalists were planning a coup d'etat and Napoleon, by virtue of being a talented outsider was entrusted with suppressing rebellion on the streets of Paris. The following morning, the 5th of October 1795, Napoleon, aged 26, ordered up 40 cannon from the suburbs and placed them in key central locations. At 4.30 p.m. a mob of 25,000 advanced on his positions to be met with a few stern broadsides. By evening Napoleon was being hailed as the saviour of the Republic. He did not look back.

While it is tempting to do likewise, I shall attempt to press on, the story of Napoleon in fact gets better. Le Petit Tondu or 'little skinhead' as he was known was made commander-in-chief of the army of the interior. He took to roaming the streets of Paris where one day a fishwife took him to task along the following lines: 'What do you politicians care if we starve as long as you get fat?' Boney, for he certainly was, replied 'Look at me, mother, and say which of us is thinner.'

While Paris convulsed with laughter and *bonhomie*, Napoleon married the dusky Josephine and slipped off two days later to command the offensive against Italy. He told his men: 'Soldiers, you are naked, badly fed... Rich provinces and great towns will be in your power and in them you will find honour, glory, wealth.' Italy was very much up for grabs in those days and Napoleon grabbed it much as Charlemagne had done a thousand years previous-

CONTINUED

61

ly. Ever on the lookout for good P.R., Napoleon strode up the steps of Milan Cathedral one afternoon and pinned a note on the door with his dagger. 'People of Italy,' it ran, 'I, Napoleon, offer you your freedom.' Such modesty and restraint were not to last – eight years later it was a case of 'We, Napoleon'.

In 1798 England was the only remaining fly in the French ointment jar. Napoleon was appointed to lead an invasion. After a rapid troop inspection he came up with an unusual plan for our downfall – attack Egypt. The so-called Directors of France were delighted to get rid of the skinhead superstar and off he went.

Napoleon liked Egypt and thought of becoming a Moslem. Everything was going swimmingly until one Admiral Horatio Nelson arrived unannounced and wiped out the French fleet. Napoleon was trapped. He marched around the Middle East for a while trying it on against the Syrians and Turks, then he heard that France had taken a lurch to the left and was ripe for a monarchist coup. Napoleon left his Egyptian army, hot-footed it back to Paris and within a month of his return had toppled the government and taken over. He was thirty years old, a national hero and the undisputed number one Frenchman. It was time to move into property development.

Piles were not the only reason Napoleon couldn't sit still for long, he was also a workaholic. Napoleon's Albert Speer was a man named Fontaine with whom he used to cruise Paris having brainwaves. Over the next decade the pair put up a large number of grandiose buildings, not to mention hospitals, embankments, bridges, fountains, columns, monuments, gardens, streets, canals, markets, slaughterhouses, granaries, sewers, museums, public baths, libraries as well as

A NATION OF SHOPKEEPERS.
TELL THE MEN!

the odd Arc de Triomphe. Millions of francs were spent on the Louvre which became a vast trophy house of looted exotica. Napoleon wanted continual progress reports on each and every project. He scrutinized the accounts, interfered, bullied and issued orders and decrees like some possessed Dalek.

CONTINUED

When he got tired of rearranging the view from his Tuileries Palace window he laid into reforming the French education system, the law, the church, the press, the theatre. He established the Banque de France, the *Legion d'Honneur* and, having dipped his ambitious fingers into these and other pies, he could always return to his favourite pastime, playing soldiers.

Napoleon at Waterloo (circa quarter past six)

The rest of Europe wasn't over keen on Napoleon and his *Grande Armée*. Its tendency to win decisive battles may have been a factor here. England in particular was less than thrilled to see a French Empire controlling the coast from Antwerp to Genoa and then declare a blockade against British ships and goods. We plotted with anyone who would listen; exiled French aristocrats, Austrians, Swedes, Portuguese and Russians. We launched campaigns in Spain and Holland, but ultimately Europe's deliverance was due to Napoleon shooting himself massively in the foot. In the spring of 1812 he set out from Poland into Russia with 435,000 men. By November less than 10,000 able-bodied soldiers remained with Napoleon's main force. Come early December not even Napoleon remained with Napoleon's force.

All this must have been pretty galling for the man who had handed out half a dozen European thrones to his family; to the victor of Marengo, Ulm, Jena, Austerlitz and Wagram; to the man who'd been voted Consul for life by a ratio of 600 to 1, gone on to run for Emperor and who at the critical moment of the ceremony in Notre Dame had snatched the crown from the Pope and placed it on his own head. But was Napoleon a broken man as he sped back to Paris? Did his mind dwell on the freezing horrors of a campaign where a quick kip inside a horse's carcass was considered luxury? No Sir.

After a non-stop, two week journey he went straight into consultation with his ministers. '... I was in Moscow. I thought I could sign a peace. I stayed there too long. I made a very big mistake but it is one I shall be able to repair.' And patch things up he very nearly did. With raw conscripts he

CONTINUED

held at bay assaults on all France's frontiers; the problem was the French. They seemed to have lost their appetite for *'la gloire'* and while Napoleon was at the front dealing it out to the Austrians and Prussians, his ministers opened talks with the enemy and made moves to wheel out a new Louis. The rest, as they say, is history. Abdication, attempted suicide, exile on Elba, the dramatic return, the Hundred Days, Waterloo, St Helena. Napoleon died at the age of fifty-one, grumbling about the English and their 'hired assassins'.

While it would be churlish to deny his greatness, one should never forget the fact of his Corso-Italian origins. A thousand years before, the Emperor Charlemagne had occasioned a rush of blood to the French head – away from the French stomach one imagines. According to this timetable France will be trying it on again sometime around 2800 AD. Who, one wonders, will be the next to make a French plaything of continental Europe, to bring back *gloire* to the Loire… a Frenchman, perhaps?

> Frenchmen are like grains of gunpowder – each by itself smutty and contemptible, but mass them together and they are terrible indeed.
> SAMUEL TAYLOR COLERIDGE

COMING SOON
FRENCH
ROCK 'N' ROLL

The Famous
FRENCH

NUMBER 5:
Edouard Brassière,
1799–1851

A schoolteacher from Bayonne whose hobby was metalwork and whose obsession was the female anatomy. He designed his first 'chest enforcer' for his mother, Josephine. She refused to wear it after the wire began to rust so Edouard experimented with models made of copper and even gold.

'A heaving bosom is like a dangerous criminal, it must be securely contained,' was one of his maxims. Another ran: 'Show me a woman whose breasts are identical and I will go down into the valley.'

Heroes
OF THE REPUBLIC

General de Gaulle, 1890–1970

Under the French law of 1881 it is an offence to insult the President of the Republic. De Gaulle invoked this law on numerous occasions. In Britain we consider it a cornerstone of our democracy to be able to insult anyone we wish. Mindful of this and notwithstanding the menace to my personal safety posed by the French secret 'service', I offer you ten little-known facts about Charles de Gaulle: the awkward bugger with the silly hat and the giant nose.

1. In August 1940 de Gaulle was sentenced to death by the French.
2. De Gaulle had a lifelong passion for Tizer.
3. General de Gaulle was the second Frenchman ever to use a biro.
4. In July 1961 de Gaulle urinated on the Finnish ambassador from the top of the Eiffel Tower.
5. De Gaulle received no credit either as a lyricist or session musician on Lou Reed's *Transformer* album.
6. General de Gaulle once had an orgasm in Notre Dame.
7. President de Gaulle was known to the nation as *Tante Yvonne*.
8. President Kennedy referred to him as 'Stonewall de Gaulle'.
9. De Gaulle's great nephew Raoul runs a mobile chip shop in Brisbane, Australia.
10. Charles de Gaulle airport near Paris is *not* named after him.

French Intelligence

On Judgement Day, when the French nation is called to account for its sins, after the Dreyfus Affair and the Terror there will be no more damaging charge laid against her than that of the sinking of the Greenpeace ship, the *Rainbow Warrior*.

Ever since the Second World War, when France was nearly snuffed out for good, Claude has been terrified of being classed as a third-division power. That is why he insists on having *Appellation Contrôlée* nuclear weapons. Psychologists recognize this as the 'I've got a small willy so I'd better get a Ferrari' syndrome.

Of course there's little point in having a Ferrari unless you drive around making a lot of noise and attracting everyone's attention. So Claude took his nukes for a spin in the South Pacific where only a small number of primitive people would actually suffer and the rest of the world could watch this mighty display of French power. Everything was hunky-dory until Greenpeace showed up and told Claude to stop playing with his nasty toys. And Claude did not like this one little bit…

In July 1985, as the *Rainbow Warrior* was preparing to lead a flotilla of yachts towards Muroroa Atoll in protest at French nuclear weapon-testing, two bombs attached to her hull sent her to the bottom of Auckland harbour. Nine people on board escaped but a Portuguese photographer, Fernando Pereira, was killed.

Shortly afterwards, a French man and woman were arrested. 'Monsieur and Madame Turenge' were travelling on Swiss passports and her address book contained telephone numbers for the DGSE, the French intelligence service. The couple were charged with murder and conspiracy to commit arson. In the course of

New Zealand's biggest-ever criminal investigation four further French suspects were sought but never captured.

The French government denied any involvement in the affair and wheeled out a former Chief of Staff to de Gaulle, one Bernard Tricot, to conduct an enquiry. After an exhaustive investigation he declared that the sinking of the ship was nothing to do with the French. It wouldn't have been in their interests to upset a friendly power, would it? 'It must have been someone else out to discredit us,' he said. Even the French public were amazed.

The Turenges – now revealed to the world as Major Alain Mafart and Captain Dominique Prieur of the DGSE – stood trial and were sentenced to ten years for manslaughter. It was not long, however, before they were released from prison in New Zealand to serve their sentences on French soil, in that well-known hell-hole, Polynesia. Here they were photographed romping in the surf and Captain Prieur was so closely confined that she became pregnant and had to return to France for medical reasons.

Relations between France and New Zealand have never recovered from the *Rainbow Warrior*. It might just be something to do with the fact that it took the French six years to apologise, and then they didn't mean it.

INDEPENDENT 10 JULY 1991

FRENCH SNUBBED

Wellington – New Zealand will send its lowest ranking cabinet minister, Wyatt Creech, to a French Embassy celebration on Bastille Day. This follows the French announcement that the Rainbow Warrior saboteur, Colonel Alain Mafart, had been awarded the Order of Merit.

As Launched by

We French know a thing or two about military humiliation from bitter first hand experience. More importantly we know how to get even with the bastards. That's why we've put all our savoir faire into the amazing new generation, sea-skimming **EXOCET BONJOUR** – the World's first FLYING SUPPOSITORY.

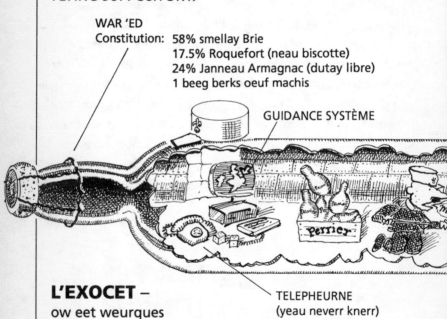

WAR 'ED
Constitution: 58% smellay Brie
17.5% Roquefort (neau biscotte)
24% Janneau Armagnac (dutay libre)
1 beeg berks oeuf machis

GUIDANCE SYSTÈME

L'EXOCET –
ow eet weurques

TELEPHEURNE
(yeau neverr knerr)

Catch 'em with their pants down and ram home the advantage. Fire and forget but don't forget to fire! Oil tankers, warships, even skyscrapers start to tremble when you say *'Bonjour'* with an Exocet. When it comes to Le Crunch you may be a third rate power but you no longer have to come third.

Shiites

LEETLE WEENGS
(pulled oeuf ze petit sparreux)

LE FIZZAY PERRIER for ewmph

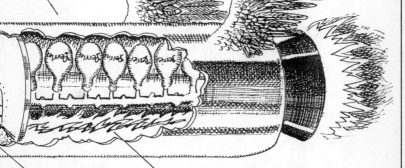

LE CHICKEN SHEET

CHAMBRE DE COMBUSTION

✂

Le Sport

This section will not detain you long, dear reader. Are there many French sporting legends whose deeds have helped to forge the nation's sense of self? Is there an impressive list of French Olympic Champions? Has France ever won the football World Cup? Has France a dazzling history of world-beating golfers, boxers, tennis-players? The answer is a resounding *Non*. OK, so they had Georges Carpentier (remember him?) and they've still got that prancing dandy Henri Leconte but, all in all, the *beurre* is spread pretty thin.

That, however, is not the real charge that France has to answer. Any sports devotee can sympathize with a third-rate sporting nation *provided they play fair*. And that, of course, is where François shows his true colours for he is a *poor loser*. Take the French rugby team. What a collection of whingers and back-stabbers, temperamentally unable to accept defeat, constantly complaining of conspiracies by Anglo-Saxon referees and players. The world recognizes them for what they are – a shabby collection of poor sportsmen, many of them dredged up from jails and back alleys and turned loose in blue shirts to ply their skills as thugs and muggers on the pitch.

Of course, there is a simple reason for this deficiency. They don't play cricket. If they did their history would be nobler and they would not revere the absurd *Tour de France*. Whoever heard of an event whose cherished prize is a yellow jersey? Only in Gaul...

Great Moments
IN FRENCH HISTORY

PART 5: THE MAGINOT LINE

In the 1920s and 30s several countries built elaborate fortifications designed to make invasion a thing of the past. The largest and most sophisticated of these defensive walls was constructed by the French and named after André-Louis-René Maginot, Minister of War 1929–31. The Maginot Line ran the entire length of the French-German border. It featured thick concrete, heavy and retractable guns, underground railways and established strongholds. Air-conditioning and recreation areas were provided for the troops who considered it to be more comfortable than the average modern city. It was a superb engineering achievement.

Unfortunately, this mighty fortification was to prove as efficient as the buoyancy tanks on the Titanic. When the time came for the Maginot Line to be put to the test, Adolf Hitler chose not to venture across the French-German border. He invaded through Belgium.

> There's something Vichy
> about the French
> IVOR NOVELLO, 1941

Heroes

OF THE REPUBLIC

Marshal Philippe Pétain, 1856–1951

As a junior officer his confidential file was prophetically annotated thus: 'If this officer rises above the rank of Major it will be a disaster for France.' Pétain became a Colonel in 1912, was charged with defending Verdun in 1916 and the following year appointed Commander-in-Chief of the French army in the field. In the face of widespread mutinies he tried to paper over the cracks and followed a policy of appeasement. This led to the virtual elimination of France as a fighting force in the First World War. Ten days after the Armistice he was created a Marshal.

After the collapse of France in 1940 he was made Head of State – or chief puppet of the Vichy government. He held the strange belief that France could only be regenerated by suffering and took every opportunity of testing his theory. He was awarded the death penalty after the Liberation but the sentence was commuted to life imprisonment. He died in captivity.

50 *First-class*

REASONS TO HATE THE FRENCH

PART FOUR

31. Everything shuts on Monday
32. Everything stops for lunch
33. Maurice Chevalier
34. Motorway tolls
35. French driving
36. French banks
37. *Pissoirs*
38. Rabies
39. French films
40. Jacques Tati

Standby pop-pickers, French rock 'n' roll is nearly upon us

A Frenchman visits his doctor.

DOCTOR: We have the results of your tests. You have rabies. I'm sorry to tell you it may be fatal.

FRENCHMAN: In that case, bring me a pen and paper.

DOCTOR: What for? To make a will?

FRENCHMAN: No. To make a list of the people I want to bite.

Non Merci Le Rock'n'Roll

Mireille Mathieu, Didier Clapton, Charles Aznavour, le jazz-rock, Serge Gainsborough and above all Johnny Halliday. It is very easy to dismiss French music.
I hereby do so.

Heroines
OF THE REPUBLIC
Edith Cresson, 1934–

France's first female Prime
Minister and the most powerful woman in France since
Joan of Arc, though not quite
so well-educated. Catapulted
into high office by François
Mitterand, 'Edict' Cresson has
her body dressed by Saint Lau-
rent and her mind by the
Reader's Digest. History will
remember her for two remarks:
that the Japanese are 'ants' and
that a quarter of British men
are 'navigators of the windward
passage' (i.e. homosexual).
These utterances have been
interpreted to mean that the
French electronics industry is
in terminal decline and that no
steward touched her knee the
last time she flew British Air-
ways. Known as 'Madam nine-
teen per cent', a reference to
her popularity rating, she
was the Fifth Republic's
shortest-serving Prime
Minister.

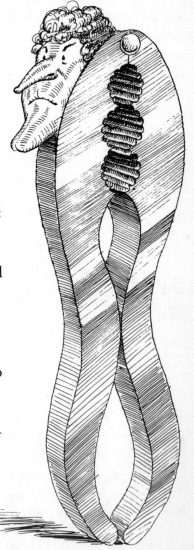

Being There

The British are intrepid explorers. Our empire, the greatest ever known, was not won by enjoying the easy life within these sacred shores. We travel and travel damn well, enduring privation and hardship, disaster and disease as if they were mere pinpricks. At hunger, pain and barbarism we do not flinch. Nowhere though is our mettle, our unflappable genius, more rigorously tested than when we venture across our moat, the English Channel, to dwell amongst the Gaul.

There are of course a number of perfectly sound reasons why an Englishman might want to mix his hash with Johnnie Gauloise. Poitiers, Crécy and Agincourt are all delightful places. One might even wish to make a tour of the Maginot Line, swinging up into Belgium and Waterloo. Travelling by means other than tank or, at the very least, armoured personnel carrier is not recommended.

If you must drive in a vehicle unprotected by Chobham armour and are thus obliged to be on the wrong side of the road, here are a few useful pointers: Claude drives like a Brazilian on dexedrine and only uses the brake when the horn has packed up. He shows as much consideration for his fellow road-users as an armed Palestinian in a crowded synagogue. It is no coincidence that Claude's progress is measured in terms of 'Kill-ometres' per hour.

A few stiff drinks before slumping behind the wheel is considered by the French to enhance their motoring prowess. This is probably true. The means of transport for which they are best suited is the hot-air balloon. In charge of anything faster, disaster cannot be far off. However, if Claude happens to drive one of the articulated shopping malls that passes for a lorry in France, he will

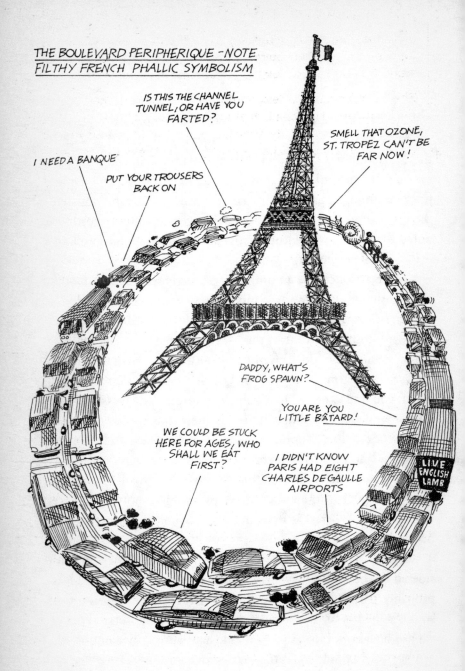

THE BOULEVARD PÉRIPHÉRIQUE

Since the French stopped using the guillotine, they've been keeping the numbers down with the aid of a ten-billion-franc Wall of Death known as Le Boulevard Périphérique.

This 'road', originally designed for the invalid carriage, encircles Paris. The idea is that instead of a bunch of maniacs crossing the city, they go round it. And indeed you do get there much quicker, provided your destination is the next world.

typically be found swilling spirits at six in the morning. Very often he climbs into the wrong cab. The resulting unfamiliarity with the controls, combined with his drunkenness and innate lack of coordination gives rise to frequent cases of what is known as 'involuntary road-widening'.

Should you be forced to interrupt your journey for food or fuel you may well find yourself at the mercy of two gangsters known as Jacques Fabre and Lesley Routier. The former runs concessions along such roads as the Autoroute du Mort and will charge you two francs for a glass of tap water. Order a steak at one of Lesley's establishments and you will quite probably be getting your first taste of horsemeat. Under no circumstances should you answer any calls of nature at either place.

And so you reach your journey's end, pondering the phrase, 'To travel is better than to arrive'. In the case of France this should be, 'To leave is better than to arrive'. You find a quiet stretch of beach, close your eyes and imagine you are back in Blighty. A foot stamps on your Adam's apple, a greasy calloused foot attached to a middle-aged delinquent wearing sunglasses and a bathing costume so inadequate as to expose its owner to the risk of sunburn of the scrotum. He and twelve of his chums have erected a volleyball net above your person, while their scrawny womenfolk are using your copy of the *Daily Telegraph* to light their barbecue.

You smile and move on past unshaven bikers comparing the length of their flick knives; geriatrics fornicating behind tattered wind-breakers; defecating children; transsexual trawlermen mending their fishnet stockings, until you reach another likely French-free zone. As your eyelids close once more, a seven-pound cannonball lands on your solar plexus. How foolish of you not to realize that boule-playing peasants running on neat Pernod regard this as their hallowed turf! A blue-overalled Quasimodo shuffles into view. He does not apologise, he merely gives that most typical of French gestures, the shrug, and accompanies it with the expression 'Bof'. When Claude says 'Bof' what he's trying to say is, '*Merde*, I dunno, it's not my fault if I'm blind in both eyes and suffer from flatulence of the elbow, I'm only a semi-civilized Frenchman with my brain up my bum, what do you expect?'

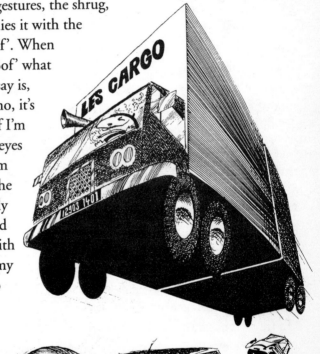

86

Heroes

OF THE REPUBLIC

Jean-Luc Godard, 1930–

One of cinema's authentic *auteurs*. He once wrote: 'I direct my films for myself. If anyone else can understand them I have failed. My eye is a camera and my brain is an editing suite. My ear is a recording studio and my foot is an usherette. I am a cinema, tickets please.'

In the happy-go-lucky days of Paris in the spring of 1956, nobody typified the polo-necked, chain-smoking, café-hopping, crap-talking Frenchman better than Jean-Luc. He once went to buy a packet of Gauloises and returned three days later with the packet unopened. 'I don't smoke,' he explained.

GO BACK 6 PAGES TO
FRENCH ROCK 'N' ROLL

A Powerful Thirst

176 million bottles of Cognac are sold in France per year as well as nine million bottles of Armagnac. For a guaranteed hangover, though, you're on safer ground with one of the 500 million bottles of grape brandy produced annually from the wine lake. Failing that, pit your brain cells against thirty million bottles of Calvados. Still parched? Try some Marc de Gewurztraminer in Alsace made from grape skins and pips.

France is the home of numerous liqueurs and spirit-based drinks, unleashing some 500 different decoctions of herbs, fruit and spice upon its liverish citizens. Johnnie Gauloise may have the appetite for good food, but how often does he taste it?

Having swallowed what has gone thus far, I'm sure it comes as no surprise for you to learn that France makes 250 types of beer. Production occurs mainly in those bits of France which have tended in the past not to be bits of France but rather of, say, Germany. Despite this head start, French beer is mostly pretty crappy – this in no way hinders Claude from drinking three and a half billion pints of the stuff per year.

If you fancy a tipple in Gaul, it has been calculated you will have 50,000 domestic labels from which to choose and that's without any 'back' vintages. Forget not that the French are big whisky drinkers and that many of their bottles carry no labels whatsoever. What does it all add up to? This... Johnnie Gauloise has the world's highest consumption of booze, equivalent to three and a half gallons of pure alcohol per person per year. The good news is that ten years ago the same figure was four gallons, which means that in a couple of centuries' time he may be nearly sober.

And this is the country where Ayatollah Khomeini spent his exile.

Heroes
OF THE REPUBLIC

Gerard Depardieu, 1948–

France's answer to Robert de Niro, he grew his nose for his acclaimed peformance in *Cyrano de Bergerac*. He is the Samson of the French film industry and, without his name somewhere in the credits, of recent years no French film has achieved a release in the English-speaking world. He is a giant of a man both physically and emotionally and seeks out roles which challenge mainstream bourgeois thinking.

He has played cripples, freaks, gays, transvestites, revolutionaries and comes up smelling of roses every time. It is rumoured that he is to star as Francois Mitterand (to Isabelle Hubert's Edith Cresson) in a new romantic comedy designed to revive the Socialist government's popularity before the next election. This could be gorgeous Gerard's first mistake.

Fantastically Annoying
FRENCH HABITS

1. Public scratching of the testes
2. Men kissing in public
3. Men kissing you
4. Horn honking
5. Telling jokes about the Belgians
6. Pretending they don't speak English
7. Waving their arms around
8. Playing volleyball on crowded beaches
9. Smoking between courses
10. Smoking Gauloises anywhere
11. Slicing through English fishing nets on the high seas
12. Trapping British holiday-makers behind barricaded juggernauts

Heroines
OF THE REPUBLIC
Edith Piaf, 1915–63

The gramophone came really   too late for Edith, as did the opening of the first Burger King restaurant in Montmartre. A slender, almost skeletal creature known as the 'Sparrow', she could nonetheless belt out a powerful vocal, none more so than her 1932 smash 'Je ne regrette rien ne va plus'. In her heyday she was the toast of Paris, the croissant of Calais and the biscotte of Bezancourt. You could buy Piaf pyjamas; eat *petit pois Piaf* and smoke Piaf ready-rubbed shag in your Piaf cigarette papers. But inevitably the Sparrow's days were numbered and now she warbles in the great nest in the sky.

Real name: Gomez Peterssen
Favourite ice cream flavour:
Double chocolate

The French Language

When it comes to swearing and swearwords the French are wholly without imagination. Their insults are nearly all locked in the bathroom, indeed many have trouble lifting themselves from the bidet. What follows may at times shock you in its crudeness as well as the contempt it displays for the human form and its necessary functions.

Younger readers are advised to move on to the next section, older ones have doubtless already done so.

CON

If you are of the opinion that a French person is being stupid (this can happen) it is odds-on you'll call him a *con*. Decency does not permit a precise translation but an English four-letter word sharing the first and third letters of the French one may spring to mind.

French	idiomatically	literally
un con	an idiot	a vagina (male)
une conne	a female idiot	a vagina (female)
déconner	to fool about	to withdraw from a vagina
connement	foolishly	vaginally
un connard	a fool	a fellow with vaginal characteristics
une connasse	a stupid woman	a great vagina
le roi des cons	a prince of fools	the king of vaginas

nous parlons Français

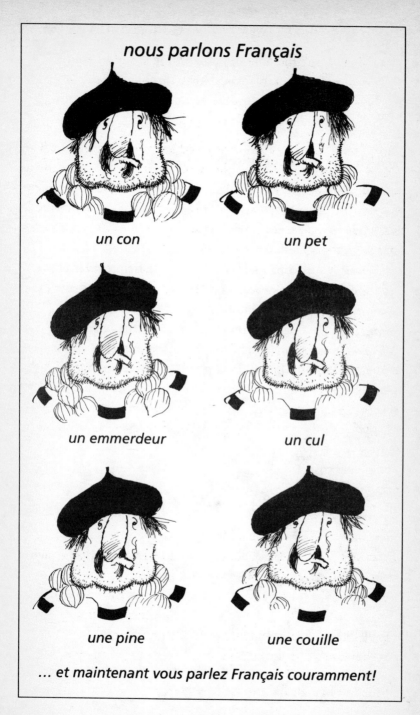

un con

un pet

un emmerdeur

un cul

une pine

une couille

... et maintenant vous parlez Français couramment!

The Mistral isn't the only thing whistling around France driving people crazy. A veritable gale blows throughout the year, malodorous and fetid – it has been calculated that at any given moment one million French people are farting.

French	idiomatically	literally
péter	to fart/to break	
un pet	a fart/a nobody	
un péteur	a farter (male)	
une péteuse	a farter (female)	
un péteux	a pauper	a frequent farter
un pétard	a firework, a reefer	something made to fart
être pété	to be smashed/stoned	to be farted
pétant l'air	self-important	farting air
pets-de-nonne	small light pastries	nuns' farts
Maréchal Pétain	Marshal Pétain	no relation

I conclude this section with a curious phrase that reveals much about French attitudes to punctuality: *je te verrais à huit heures pétantes* – 'I'll see you at eight sharp' or, if you prefer, 'I'll see you at the fart of eight.'

Merde is one of the most commonly used French exclamations. From it are derived numerous expressions and spin-offs without which inter-Gallic communications would be in serious trouble.

French	idiomatically	literally
merde	golly!	shit!
merdique	disappointing	covered in shit
emmerdant	boring	dispensing shit
un emmerdeur	a tedious person	a shit spreader
un emmerdement	a foul-up/trouble	being totally covered in shit

As well as being an expression of mild surprise, *merde* can also mean 'good luck'. If you see someone about to sit an exam it is obligatory to wish them *merde*. Hence, if a Frenchie trundles up to you with a twinkle in his eye and delivers himself of the phrase *j'ai marché dans le merde avec le pied gauche* ('I've trodden in some dogshit with my left foot') do not back away, sniffing the air. What he means is 'I'm feeling lucky today.'

LE MENU GÉNITALIQUE

From fannies, farting and faeces it is but a short journey, sensitive reader, to bollocks, bums and pricks. Here is a selection of *crudités*.

French	idiomatically	literally
un cul	an arse	
c'est un vrai cul	he's a real arse	
un culcul	an arse and a half	
d'avoir la bouche en cul de poule	to have a mouth like a chicken's bottom	to be tight-lipped
une pine	a penis	
un pinard	(a bottle of) wine	a phallic object
pinailler	to nit pick	to use one's penis as a sword
un pinailleur	a quibbler	one who practises such swordsmanship
une couille	a testicle	
mes couilles!	come off it!	my testicles!
tu es une couille molle	you're a pushover	you're a soft testicle
il y a une couille dans le potage	something's wrong	there's a testicle in the soup

> If the French were really intelligent, they'd speak English
>
> WILFRED SHEED

What ARE
<u>They Going On About</u>

*T*here's nothing Claude enjoys more, particularly when he's eating, than a wide-ranging and empassioned argument. Frenchmen have firmly held opinions about virtually everything. What they believe is immaterial (and usually crap): it is the unshakeability of their beliefs and the noise they employ in defending them that counts.

Some have argued that talking and eating is an efficient way for the Frenchman to achieve the indigestion he seeks. Others hold that his jaw muscles are so over-developed that regular exercise is needed to prevent them becoming painful. Either way the result tends to be a release of hot air on a Montgolfiesque scale.

Much of the blame for this national pastime of futile debate can be laid at the door of René Descartes – Rennie to his friends – a lovely little seventeenth century thinker. Rennie started out being a bit of a Doubting Thomas. 'If you can't prove what you say scientifically I refuse to believe it,' was his early line. Such was his scepticism that Rennie had all but stopped believing in himself and we might never have heard from him again but then, one day he came up with a pithy little three worder that's had philosophers on the edge of their seats ever since. *Cogito ergo sum*. I think I have the urge to be a sumo wrestler.

Thinking away hard at about the same time was young Blaise Pascal. Blaise came up with an ingenious piece of sophistry known as Pascal's Wager which states: 'If there is a God then there must be a possibility of facing infinite suffering in hell. So, it is rational to act as though God does exist, however low the probability, since the resulting sacrifice of pleasure is only finite.' How many converts to the faith this argument has yielded we do not know.

Then of course there was Poisson. Siméon-Denis Poisson to be precise, the noted mathematical physicist of the 1820s and 30s. Contrary to popular belief he did not invent the fish finger. Rather, he left to future generations Poisson's Theorem of Numbers from which we learn that the more often you toss a coin, the more likely you are to get a 50/50 heads-tails result. French society was transformed.

Skipping lightly over such colossal intellects as the monkish Pierre Abelard; Henri Bergson with his double view of time; Nicholas Malebranche who believed we see the world only through ideas, we arrive at the mirrored doors of Existentialism. Now these guys could think you under the table. They thought right through the Second World War and then thought some more for luck.

What is Existentialism? Good question, can you take a couple of weeks off? Well, they see a different type of being applying to Man than to things. They believe that Man can be active and creative while things cannot. Man has choice. He must choose and furthermore must choose the principles on which he chooses.

Although a non-driver himself, Jean-Paul Sartre was an ardent fan of formula one motor racing. He was also, as Simone de Beauvoir would tell him most mornings, a chain smoker and a failure at brushing his teeth. One day at La Coupole he thought up a brilliant scheme that would net him free cigarettes for life and a pit pass at every grand prix. 'They will name a brand of cigarettes after me,' he declared. 'The packet shall be black and gold. Then, in case there are one or two who have not switched to Jean-Paul Sartre's, they will build a beautiful car that will win all the grand prix.'

Jean-Paul peddled his idea round all the major tobacco companies only to be cruelly rebuffed. Then one day when he was watching the start of the Monaco Grand Prix, the awesome John Player Special turbo rolled out to pole position on the grid. Sartre put an axe through the television set. 'The English bastards,' he cried. 'They have stolen my idea, my colours, my designs... *merde* they have robbed me of my initials.'

My second favourite existentialist and a good buddy of JPS was Maurice Merleau-Ponty. We are all familiar of course with his phenomenological description of the phenomenum of consciousness but how many of us realize that it was as far back as 1945 that he produced his seminal *Sens et Nonsens*?

Why They Hate us

Why do the French hate the English? Jealousy, pure and simple. Claude is green-eyed with envy because of our history, our dominant language, our footballing skills, our Stock Exchange, but most of all because of our indomitable nobility of character.

A certain Dr Alphonse Bagnoles has made a study of these matters. I quote: 'A particularly bitter pill for the French to swallow was the fact that their Roman masters considered British wine to be vastly superior to the products of any Gallic vineyard. Indeed the word vinegar was first coined in Burgundy, close to where we now discover the sacred slopes of Nuits St Georges.'

Travelling back into pre-historic times, the good doctor tells us: 'Some 6,000 years ago England and France were physically linked by a narrow causeway. When this umbilical cord was severed by the forces of Nature, the French apparently were in such

---

Why Other People Hate Them Too

THE GERMANS

'The French are a bunch of losers from way back, only you British have invaded them more often. They must love it or something, why else build that ridiculous Maginot Line. After a while though it gets boring, like shooting fish in a barrel or as we say in Bavaria, like eating gateaux in the Black Forest.'

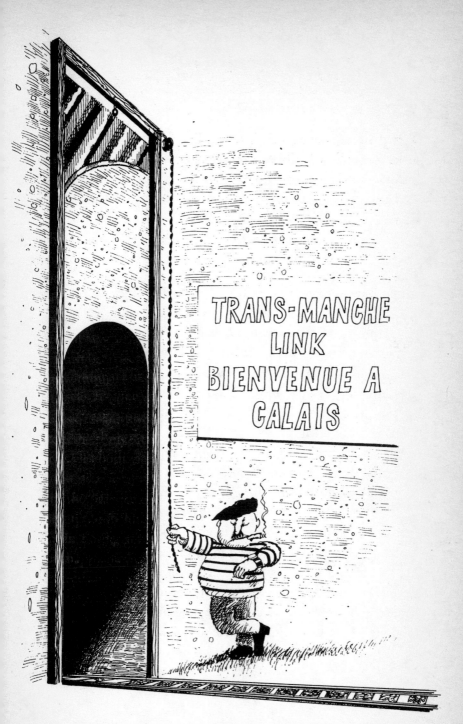

acute distress that large numbers threw themselves into the watery breach in an orgy of pre-Canutian defiance.'

Returning to the present, Dr Bagnoles identifies two factors which determine the degree of hatred felt by any particular son of Gaul towards his long-lost English cousins. He claims firstly that the animosity felt by a random Frenchman towards the English is a direct function of his proximity to England. Thus a citizen of Calais is more likely to detest the English than say a Lyonnais. The latter in turn will register a higher Anglophobe rating than an inhabitant of Marseille. By the time you get down to Corsica, where one might sensibly have imagined Albion-loathing to be part of the syllabus, you find nothing stronger than indifference. Indeed per capita sales of the Wellington boot* are higher on this rugged and beautiful island than in Royal Gloucestershire.

The second factor is perhaps even more depressing, when seen in the context of mankind's future aboard our ever-shrinking planet. Alphonse Bagnoles' researches lead him to believe that the more French an Englishman is able to speak, the more likely it is he will be misdirected, ripped off or in some way *emmerded* by the

*Source – *Institut de l'Information Chiropodique*, 75005 Paris.

typical Frenchman. God preserve the Oxford professor of modern languages on a day trip to Boulogne.

'S'il vous plaît, monsieur, je cherche le hoverport.'
'Hein, quoi?... Zut, beng salaud... Bof.'

Dr B makes one exception to these rules and that concerns the citizens of Paris. 'No one is ruder to his fellow man than a Parisian,' he states. 'He hates his fellow Parisians, loathes all other Frenchmen, but above all others he abominates the English.' Enough of theory. Let us now move on to the practice of Anglo-enragement as perfected by the denizens of France's capital.

Picture, if you will, a French bank. You negotiate the elaborate airlock door system and humbly enter the inner sanctum. There you are greeted by the sight of a fellow countryman behaving in a decidedly un-English fashion. The poor chap is weeping. He implores you to leave the bank forthwith. It is the sort of warning you have seen in a hundred horror films. 'Don't open the tomb. Don't take that modelling job with the hunchback at the wax museum. Promise me you won't swim in the Black Lagoon.' But like a hundred Hollywood heroes you know better.

'OK if I countersign these traveller's cheques?' you enquire of an unusually beautiful bank-teller.

'*Bien sûr, monsieur.*' You feel positively cheerful as the young lady coaxes the correct sounds from her computer, tears off the printout and lays it neatly astride a crisp pile of francs.

'Erm... it seems to say here that you've taken twenty-five francs commission.'

'*Oui, monsieur.*'

You mention the fact that just yesterday you paid a commission of only seven francs on an identical transaction.

'Ah *monsieur*, but that was at another bank.'

It is then explained to you that this bank charges lower commissions than any other bank in Paris, the one slight fly in the

Why Other People Hate Them Too

THE MURAUURAURUARUARUA ATOLL ISLANDERS

'When somebody comes along, bulldozes your house, rapes your wife, causes death and disease in your children and then starts testing hydrogen bombs on your beach, it can be hard to think of them as your benefactors.'

'France has made us the Kurds of the Pacific.'

ointment being that you need to exchange a sum of money so vast as to necessitate the hiring of armed security personnel.

'So,' you reason, 'if I cash another cheque or two now, you won't charge me any more commission?'

'*En principe, monsieur, non.*'

You sign two more cheques before she can change her mind and watch her enter the numbers into that which must be obeyed. Bad news. Your file has already been submitted, checked, approved and stored and is now closed. It is a highly efficient system she assures you, manufactured and designed in France. *Malheureusement*, a new file means a new commission.

'I want my cheques back, all of them.'

'But you have signed them, *monsieur*, they are now *partie du système.*'

'No they're not, I can see them on your desk.'

'But this desk is also part of the system.'

'Give me my cheques back or I'll report them stolen.'

She goes to the manager.

The manager speaks impeccable English. If you want your cheques back there will be a sixty franc *annulation* charge. No, there wasn't any discretion he could exercise in the matter. Yes, the system was far from perfect. No, he wasn't an overgrown mouse, merely doing a difficult job the best he could. You feel like Hercules trying to deal with a seven-headed Gorgon with a penknife.

'*Monsieur*,' he appeals to you, 'we can't just go back to the old-fashioned way.'

'*Monsieur*,' you reply, 'if this was the Bronze Age you and your bank would be considered old-fashioned.'

Two new customers enter the bank. Happy people, full of innocence and good intentions. They are English and brandishing traveller's cheques.

'If I were you,' you mention casually, 'I'd cash those cheques around the corner. This place is going up sometime in the next three minutes.'

'Oh yeah,' they say. 'Well, we're looking for a bit of excitement as it happens.'

Why Other People Hate Them Too

THE KURDS

'Except for the US and the Soviets, no country has done more than France to arm Saddam Hussein with efficient and terrible means of killing us'

50
First-class
REASONS TO HATE
THE FRENCH
PART FIVE

41. They give in to terrorists
42. Their bread doesn't keep
43. Their toilets are disgusting
44. They hunt wild boar
45. They won't cook you a well-done steak
46. They started the Vietnam War
47. They kidnapped Jane Birkin
48. They granted asylum to the Ayatollah Khomeini
49. They go mad on the roads in August
50. They are cannibals – they eat frogs!

Heroes
OF THE REPUBLIC

Monsewer Eddie Gray, 1922–69

The comedian who performed with the Crazy Gang. He was not French, which accounts for the fact that he was very funny.

The Famous
FRENCH

NUMBER 6:
Bernard Comte de Tampon,
1874–1938

The Tampon family were enobled during the reign of Louis XIV for their services to obstetrics. Thierry Tampon, Bernard's great-great-grandfather considered himself as much a farmer as a doctor: 'I merely harvest the fruit of the Sun King's loins.'

Bernard's attempts to enter the family business did not start well. He was expelled from medical school for missing too many periods. If the truth be known he found it hard to leave his lodgings without being accosted by desperate women who, believing in the magic of the Tampon name, would raise their skirts and swoon as he drew near. Being entirely unqualified, the only remedy Bernard could provide for these ladies' distress was both vigorous and unethical.

Soon young Bernard became addicted to the practice of fornication, but the queues outside his house grew too long and threatened public order. Thus it was, to keep the hordes at bay, he invented the device that bears his name. How happy he would be to know that decades later his brainchild succeeds in penetrating millions of women simultaneously.

*Monsieur Tampon, undaunted despite the teething problems
exhibited by the MkI version of the sanitary device
which bears his name*

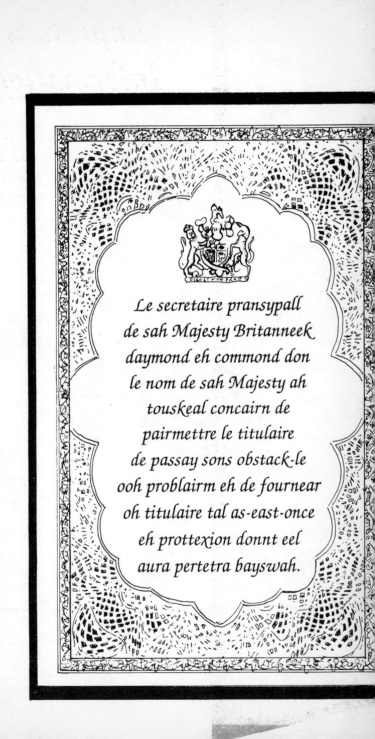

Le secretaire pransypall
de sah Majesty Britanneek
daymond eh commond don
le nom de sah Majesty ah
touskeal concairn de
pairmettre le titulaire
de passay sons obstack-le
ooh problairm eh de fournear
oh titulaire tal as-east-once
eh prottexion donnt eel
aura pertetra bayswah.

Important Information

*F*or those who possess the loathsome Euro-passport here, phonetically translated, is what it says at the front of a proper British job. Speak loudly and clearly, as though addressing a deaf child, and Claude will be collaborating in no time at all.

Où est le papier?
Où est le papier?
Monsieur, monsieur, je vais manure
Où est le papier?

La Marseillaise,
robust English version